Investing For kids

Learn how to start Earning, Saving, Investing, and watch your money grow

By Daphne M Cooper

This book belongs to

____

Table of Contents

Introduction 7

   Can I Earn Money? 7

   Isn't Making Money for Grownups? 8

   Not Everything is THAT Easy Right? 9

   About The Author 9

Chapter 1: Understanding Money 11

   What is Money? 11

   The Importance of Money 12

      What Can Money Do for You Even as A Kid? 12

   Dark Side of Money 15

   How Much Money Is Enough? 16

      Not All Happiness Relies on Money 18

      Money Is a Great Servant. Money Is a Terrible Master! 18

Chapter 2: History of Money 19

   Where it First Started 19

      What is Bartering? 20

      What Was The First Form of Money? 21

      When Did Money Become Metal? 21

   The Growth in The Rest of The World 23

      Currency Wars 23

      How Does Money Work Now? 24

   At The End of The Day 24

Chapter 3: Earning Money 25

   Timeline of Money 25

   How can I Earn Money? 27

Chapter 4: Banking 31

   History of Banking 31

   So Where Was the First Official Bank? 32

      Visa Royal 33

      Modern Banking 33

      Merchant Banks 33

   Types of Accounts 35

Chapter 5: Safety While Earning 37

Top Rules to Stay Safe Online...38

   Keep the Information You Share Limited 38

   Keeping the Privacy Settings, You Have On 38

   Being A Safe browser 39

   A Great Way to Play It Safe, Use a VPN 39

   Be Very Careful of What You Download 39

   Choose Strong Passwords.......................................40

   Keep the Antivirus Up to Date 40

Avoiding Investment Scams...41

Verifying 43

Chapter 6: Budgeting - Learn How to Handle Your Income 44

Basics of Budgeting 44

   Note the amount of income coming in......................45

   Track the spending that you do 45

   Set The Goals..45

   Making a Plan 45

   Adjustments 46

   Never Stop Checking in 46

Why Should You Budget? 46

Chapter 7: When to Spend and When to Save 49

The Art of Self-Control 49

   Out of Sight - Out of Mind 50

   Reward Yourself for Work Accomplished 50

   Set Yourself Reminders..51

   Allow Yourself to Take a Break 51

   Turn the Tasks of "Must Do" into a "Want To" 51

   Practice Planning..52

Chapter 8: Investing Money 53

Introduction To Investing 53

Different Types of Investment.......................................54

   Bonds 54

   Stocks...55

   Mutual Funds...56

   Commodities 57

Top Tips when Making An Investment 58

Conclusion 61

My other books you will love! 64

Don't forget to grab your GIFT!!! 65

References 66

Just for You

Click here

http://daphnemcooper.com/parenting.pdf

Joining the PME Community

Looking to meet other parents that can help you on your parenting journey? If so, then check out the Parenting Made Easy (PME) Community here:

https://www.facebook.com/groups/293830159257919/

Introduction

Whenever the word investing, money or finances are mentioned, you may think it is boring. But it is certainly not boring to go shopping for shoes, toys or candy. Whizzing down the aisle, it is so fun to look at everything available, and I can bet there are quite a few things you wouldn't mind buying. But to buy items that cost more than the money you currently have in your pocket; you may need to learn a thing or two. This is why I am here to help!

Learning about finances does NOT have to be boring. It does NOT have to be complicated. And it does NOT have to be confusing or difficult. Many things in this world are just over-complicated and people tend to do that. Words are used to make facts fly over people's heads (much like Peter Pan flying to Neverland). And when you do not understand words, it is also just no fun. But here, every big word is explained, simplified and examples will be given, allowing you to picture it in your head.

Can I Earn Money?

What if there is a way you can learn to earn money? What if you can put your money in a certain place, and watch it grow? Much like planting a seed in a pot and

watching it sprout? Well, it is possible! This is called investing, and the truth about investing is that you can start at almost any age. Time can be your enemy, but it can also be your ally (Zig Ziglar Quotes). The younger you start investing, the better! Then you are friends with time, as you have plenty of it! Plenty of time to learn that sometimes putting money away can result in receiving more money a little while later. If you receive more money, you can buy something bigger and better than what you first could! (Tara Siegel, 2020).

To learn how to invest, you will have to know the basics of money. Don't worry, you won't get bored to death! Think of it this way - You are a gold miner, looking for that nugget of gold. But if you waltz into the cave, what do you think will happen?

Well, firstly, you won't be able to see anything. You do not have a torch! You will stumble about blindly. You won't even know where to go. Consider this book your torch. It lights your way to your golden nugget, but to add a bonus, I will also provide you with the tools. There is no way you are mining that gold from the rock with your bare hands. You will need a pickaxe, maybe a drill, and even wooden beams to keep the mine from falling. All this will take time (much like investing), but soon you will see a growth in the amount of money you have.

Isn't Making Money for Grownups?

It is the grownup's primary responsibility to earn money, but that does not mean you cannot learn how to! The sooner you learn, the better, because it will help you now and long into the future. I bet you have learned about habits. How good habits help you in life, and how bad habits make life hard. Learning good habits with money, learning about investing, is such an incredibly good habit that you will be forever grateful for learning it! (Booth, 2020)

And do you know what the coolest part of it all is? You are probably learning something that very few of your friends are learning! If you like competitions, consider yourself a step ahead in the game. This is because schools barely cover any of this! They focus on other subjects (such as maths, languages, and science), which although good for your education, are not so beneficial for your current piggy bank. Learning how to invest, grow your money and other matters are needed in everyday life, but schools barely brush on the topic. You will see for yourself as time goes by and you advance in grades. Again, this puts you a step ahead in the game, and everyone will be wondering why you are so savvy and wise before you even hit college!

Not Everything is THAT Easy Right?

Well, in truth, no. Some matters can be a little more difficult to grasp than others, but any difficult term or words will be explained. Any issues, rules, and subjects when it comes to investing and making money will be simplified for you, and you will not walk alone in this journey. This book will guide you every step of the way. Do not be afraid to take your time with this, read things slowly, and make sure you understand each chapter before you move on. Take notes, have fun! Try to explain things to an adult. You will find that you remember a lot more once you have to teach someone else about it. So don't hesitate to share what you have learned!

A good idea would be to work through this with a grownup. Not only can the adult brush up on some of the facts, but they can also help you apply the principles in your everyday life. Whether it be finding a good place to invest, setting money aside, and making sure you don't spend it when you shouldn't. It may also mean that they will start to learn to invest with you, making it a fun bonding time with your family member!

So, you don't have to worry, you are covered. You have the toolkit to start investing, as well as learn principles in finances that most people only learn once they receive their first paycheck. You will also have time, a valuable commodity that adults do not normally have. The more you use your time wisely, the better (perhaps even opening up time for yourself in the future).

So don't be afraid to start today, one chapter at a time. With a little bit of fun, a little bit of magic, and a little bit of work, watch your knowledge grow, and your money increase.

About The Author

Being a mother, investing is a very important aspect I am adding to my children's lives. Guiding them with this step-by-step method to prepare them for a better and brighter future. The techniques are simple and easy, and I want to share them with you just as I have shared them with my children.

I want you to make the most of your childhood, and with my knowledge and guidance, you will find yourself sailing through many of the facts. You will grow in your knowledge of money, how to grow it and how to have fun while doing it! Sure, there is not a lot of charm or sparkles that comes with money, but watching it grow, seeing your success, and being able to buy or save up for something that you want is by far an amazing feeling. Especially if you manage to conquer this on your own.

I have walked this journey with my children, and I hope to walk this journey with you. So don't hesitate! Start reading and discovering the amazing secrets of investing today.

Chapter 1: Understanding Money

Today we will be talking a little bit about money. After all, there is more to it than handing a couple of dollar bills to someone in exchange for food or toys, or gadgets. To understand money, you just have to dig a little deeper. Consider this as the first step into discovering the gold nuggets hidden deep within the cave.

Now before we continue, there is just one thing you need to understand. Money can be both a terrible and a wonderful thing. It depends entirely on your approach to getting it. It can either be your master or it can be your servant. Which one do you believe is better?

If you prefer it to be your servant, you are correct. Because money is an excellent servant, but a terrible master (Barnum, Forbes). Therefore, you need to promise now at the very beginning that you will not let money control you. Money is not a supervillain in a movie, but in real life, it may as well be. There are many cases where people have done extremely bad things for money. However, those people (being the superhero of finances) thrived and decided to make money their servant. So now that you understand that money can be both good and bad, let us take a look at the role money plays in people's lives - including yours!

What is Money?

So what exactly is money? In simplest terms, it is a form of exchange. You exchange a certain amount of money for a laptop, or even something as simple as a bag of apples. Money is used to discover the value of something. After all, people do not fight so hard in competitions unless 1 million dollars was worth something to them.

Money allows you to buy things, whether it be online or at the shops, but to buy items with money - you will need to get money in the first place. Normally, your parents give you money (or you work for it), but at the end of the day, where do your parents get your money?

Apparently, your parents work for it! Do you know why people need to work for money? Well, in the olden days, people used to trade and barter. This meant that people traded their skills or products for others (Anderson, 2021). This is all good and well, except if you want to trade a table for some bread. How would this work? The table has more value than bread, but you cannot just chop a table in pieces. Now, normally a system could get set up where the baker owes bread for the table for the next three weeks. As this matter is unreliable, the written value system was established where traders used to write values on a piece of paper. People accept these values, and that was the creation of money. It was meant to solve the differences in value for different services and products! Now isn't that neat?

The Importance of Money

This brings back the question of how important money is. Well, to answer this question, it is best to ask, what exactly can money do for you? A good example is to think why pirates spent their lives in dangerous seas hunting for treasure? Well, naturally, it can have them buy a better ship, it can let them buy land, it can let them buy better weapons, etc. So now it is best to ask the question:

What Can Money Do for You Even as A Kid?

Money gives you a lot of freedom. This is clear for both kids and adults. Money allows you to do things that you want, where you want and whenever you want. Enough money can even allow you to leave a job you sorely dislike and you do not have to rely on anyone else for financial support. And as you are younger, money can help support your hobbies, your education and other matters that you may enjoy. For example, if you are an artist, you need some money for a pencil and paper. If you want to play the guitar, then you need money to buy the instrument and guitar lessons. If you want to go to school, then you need money to pay for the school.

Money can also give you choices

Nothing is more fun than being able to choose something that you want. Just choose flavor ice cream, or whether or not you want to visit someone. Having the choices is truly the best feeling in the whole wide world. But if you are stuck, and have no money, you can see your options slowly but surely getting less and less. That is no fun at all; many adults dread this very thought. So, if you have the options, it can come as a great relief.

When you have enough money, you should choose what you usually want or do not want to do. When you are older, if you want to change or quit your job, it would be good to have money for survival. If you want to travel to different countries - then the money is a must. If you want to go on vacation and buy yourself ice cream at the seaside, that costs money too.

Money gives you financial security

This may or may not be a strange idea. It is scary to think about whether or not you have money, but there are chances you do know a little of what it actually feels like. Financial security just reduces a lot of the stress in a person's life as well as your relationship with your family. Having money can lift a massive burden. You may not have to pay bills today, but when you get older, you will understand that money can help you pay the bill as well as provide security that you know when your next meal is coming (All4kids, 2021).

Having money just makes life easier for a family, as financial security can remove a lot of stress in people's lives.

Money can allow you to have more fun

Everyone knows you need money to experience a lot of fun things in life. Riding on a rollercoaster or taking a hike at the park. Money can truly allow you to experience the best of things. Whether or not it is getting a fancy PlayStation or even going  on a trip to the zoo! You can experience a lot of what life has to offer. This is sad, but a somewhat helpful tip about the day and age we now live in.

Money can also allow your family to give more

Money can teach you how to learn good living and work ethic. Many people who do not necessarily spoil their children in riches, but teach them how to work for it, allow them to forge their path into a wealthier life (Hayes, 2021). Many parents send their children to school with barely any money with this in mind. Education gives you the great opportunity to learn how to earn money.

That is why it is so important to study for those tests! They are not there to make your life miserable. They are there to allow you to learn how to earn money. It may seem odd but learning how to work out maths gives you a great advantage when you work on your finances later in life! Learning about biology can get you an education as a scientist and a nice paycheck.

Keep in mind, it is best to choose a career for yourself in the future that you will enjoy. That will give you the motivation to work harder and earn more. So, take your time during your school years to discover what you enjoy. It will get you very far.

Money does allow you to give back

At a certain point and time in your life, you can even learn to give back to those who do not have the money. Especially if you start earning money a lot sooner and a lot younger. You can help a local charity or even a certain cause which you would like to support. Great happiness comes from lending a helping hand to people who are less fortunate than you (Santi, 2017). Who knows, you may even inspire others to follow in your footsteps. That sounds a lot like being a superhero, doesn't it?

Dark Side of Money

Unfortunately, in every story, there is a villain. The same can be said for the money. You can use the money for so much good. For yourself, your family, and your community. But remember that sometimes there are a few bad things that come along with money. You have to be very careful! Especially at your age, it may be hard to realize. But as you grow older, it will become more and more obvious how people have been affected by the dark side of money. This is when people allow money to be their master and they be its servant. We do not want that, oh no! Remember! You are the master of money, not the other way around! You control the crown, and the throne, and it must remain so! Here are some common warning signs of an attack on the dark side of money!

First of all, money obsession can cause problems. This happens when money is all people can think about. You cannot get away from it. People who try to search for money and think about it all the time will just bring trouble and problems into their

lives. It will cause them to do things they shouldn't do, and to fail in other matters where they shouldn't fail (Carlson, 2021).

When money is all that, you are thinking about, then you know you are doing something wrong. You can focus on earning money or learning about it. But make sure it is not what you are always thinking about getting. Remember, the more obsessed you are, the more, bad things could happen. So, although it is good to think about money and what it can do for you, take a step back and think, "Is money controlling me? Or am I controlling it?" It should be quite easy to get an answer. Even if it is from you or the thoughts of others. The point is, if you obsess too much over money, you are not going to enjoy life.

Making money can cause more stress. This is what you need to be very careful about even at your age. Even if you lose money, do not let it bring you down. Money can bring some unwanted stress for people who believe that they are not getting enough money and they should always have more. This is the kind of thinking people have when they gamble. Most of the time, they will lose their money then (helpguidewp et al., 2021).

Start thinking about it like this: be happy with what you have and see what you can improve. Simple & Easy! You want to earn money because you want to learn how to work with finances. You want to learn to invest because you want to see the money grow. It must not be forced, and do not form a second thought that you need more. If you have a bed to sleep in, food to eat, and clothes to wear as well as education, then you have enough. So, by the end of the day, you want to earn money because you can, and it is the wise thing to do. It is not because you have to, because as of right now, depending on where you are in life, you do not have that pressure just quite yet. This makes it easier for you to control money. After all, if you lose it, it is not the end of the world. You can learn from your mistakes and try again.

How Much Money Is Enough?

This is a good question. A lot of people just think 1 million dollars! Others may consider that having enough money to pay the bills is ok. For you that is just starting, any money that you have is enough. After all, you are learning how to use the money. You do not need the

pressure of what will happen if I do not earn enough? At least, not yet anyway.

Again, it is great to set a goal to see if you can reach it. If you have 5 dollars in your pocket, buy some candy and sell it at school, then you have $20. It may not be enough to buy a cell phone, but it is certainly enough for you right now. Because you have learned how to earn an extra $15. Then if you decide to grow and expand that is up to you. But even now, do not let your love of money cause you to:

- Hurt people - this is the first rule of the game. You are forbidden to be mean!
- Move away from good friends and family - do not cut yourself off from anyone, especially people who can help you walk this journey!
- Take too much time out of your studies.
- Take too much time from your family.
- Sacrifice your time to enjoy normal activities and sports.

To bring back the example of a miner, you normally never mine on your own. You have a buddy to come with you. If your buddy tells you that you are going too deep, or it is getting too dangerous. What is the best thing you can do? Well, that is to pull back of course! You don't want to get hurt when digging for gold. The same can be said for money. You do not want to get hurt while learning how to work with money. Otherwise, a game that was once fun is now spoiled. And this relies entirely upon your attitude of what you want to do and learn.

Rather, follow the instructions that are given to you. Even if you only mine a small nugget at first, you at least now know how to mine. When you get older, you can focus on going a little deeper without having that fear of safety. The same can be said about money. You can learn a lot about money now, which will help you in the future. Imagine being able to make more money than your friends before you even hit college! Isn't that just amazing?

Not All Happiness Relies on Money

This is just a good reminder here and now that not all happiness relies on how much money you can make (Dunn & Courtney, 2021). Of course, it is good to have financial goals at your age. It is perfect to learn how to make your budget. It is fantastic to grow the amount of money you have. This is never a bad thing!

But then again, don't get addicted to the idea that money can buy you happiness. Your family and friends should remain important. Remember, you have time to learn how to make money, and you do not have such excessive pressure of failing. So this is a good time to learn how to make money, but you never, ever want to let money have a massive impact on you. I'm gonna say it again, and you are going to say it with me:

Money Is a Great Servant. Money Is a Terrible Master!

If there is anything you can and should learn from this chapter, it is this fact. Because money can do a lot for you. That part is obvious. Money plays an important role in many people's lives. That is also a fact. But allowing yourself to be the superhero rather than the villain when it comes to money is your choice. So, which one will you choose? The right side, or the dark side?

Furthermore, do not be afraid of what you can and cannot do. There may be many suggestions, and it would be best to ask an adult to try these activities. After all, if you do not understand something, or are a little scared to try it out on your own, it is best to have someone with you that has spent time and hours working with money.

Making money is not necessarily easy. Investing is not easy either, but learning from the start can truly boost your success in the future. Worries about overspending and not being able to meet your bills will become a matter of the past.

Chapter 2: History of Money

So naturally, there is a start to everything right? A chicken comes from an egg for example. There was the start of a paper airplane too. Someone folded a piece of paper with hopes that it would fly into the air. There is even a beginning of a computer, and cell phones. Everything has a beginning, and the same can be said for money. So how exactly did money begin? Now that is a very good question. Well, money started to solve a problem, and we will be looking at that in-depth with this chapter.

Where it First Started

Money can be anything. It can be represented by that of a metal coin, a piece of paper (what you may be familiar with), or even something as simple as a shell! So tell me, why do you think that you can trade a couple of shells for a loaf of bread?

Well, that is because people place value on it! It is used as a form of exchange and allows people to choose the value of their items and services. For instance, a loaf of bread is going to be cheaper than television. How do you know that? Well, because of the amount of money it costs! Do you think you can buy a television with the same amount of money as a loaf of bread? Of course not! That is just silly! But this allows you to see that money has value because people believe that it does - which is why money works all too well.

But throughout history, you can imagine that money has changed. We aren't carrying around our bags of gold to buy a house. Nor taking seashells to our grocery store. Things have changed over time, and to appreciate money, it is best to take a deep look into its history. Don't be afraid! It is quite an easy journey and fun facts that you can share with your friends. Now you can truly answer the question of: where did money come from?

Believe it or not, money has been in existence for the last 3,000 years (Beattie, 2021). That means the idea and invention of money is over 3,000 years old! That is how many great-grandfathers for you? Don't worry, you don't need to figure that one out.

But before the money had been used so many years ago, there was likely to be a system of bartering. However, keep in mind, this is a guess...a logical guess, but still a guess from historians. What are historians? People who study history and work out what happened in the past. They are the ones who believed that bartering was used before money. And it does make sense.

What is Bartering?

Bartering happens when you trade a good or service for another good or service. For example, you trade your cow's milk for some eggs. Or you can specifically exchange a bushel of grain for a pair of shoes. But whenever these arrangements are made, they would take an immense amount of time. For example, if you had an axe you wanted to trade for some meat and skin of a mammoth, you

would search and find someone who would be willing to take the axe and help hunt down this enormous creature. However, if the people do not like this deal, then you may want to change the deal, adding more for what they believe to be worth the risk (Corporate Finance Institute, 2021).

Over time, history has shown that different currencies (forms of money) were starting to grow. It normally involved items that could very easily be traded to and through, such as salt, weapons, and animal skins. This developed over time as more and more people started making discoveries. Naturally, a wooden spear turned into a spear with an iron tip, etc. These items were good forms of exchange, but how valuable they were to a person was still relatively debatable.

When Money was introduced, it rapidly increased the speed of transactions. You know how long it can take standing at a till waiting for your turn to pay. Now imagine, some of these trades could very well take hours, to even days depending on the situation!

What Was The First Form of Money?

In 1,200 BC Cowrie Shells - a shell of a prominent and widely available mollusk was used as money - specifically in China in the period of the Shang Dynasty. The beauty of the shells was its near impossibility to forge them (after all, who could go out and create a shell?) However, the shell was not just used in China, but 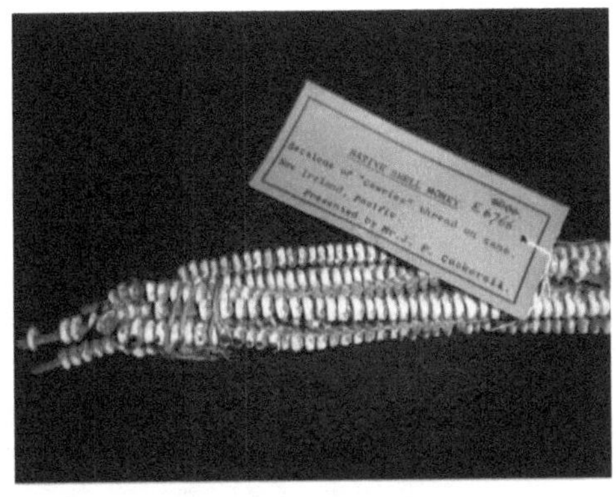 other societies in Africa and even India made use of the cowries. This is because it was used the longest, and many people used them! It may as well have been as popular then as the US dollar is today! Imagine that! Money out of seashells! Do you think you could carry around a bunch of seashells in exchange for some food or toys? (Honick, 2021)

When Did Money Become Metal?

The cowrie shells acted as an inspiration. China started to create bronze as well as copper cowrie shell look-alikes in 1000 BC. This could be considered as one of the very earliest forms of metal coins. They then developed into round coins - the base was completely made of metal and even contained holes so that they could be strung together like a chain (NOVA Online, n.d.).

Taking a peek outside of China, many Greek cities of Iona started designing coins for the use of the business. The place that started it all was called Sardis which was the capital city of Lydia (or what you now know as Turkey!) And believe it or not, the coins looked a lot like the coins we know and see today! (Honick, 2021)

Naturally, once one thing was invented, as time passed by, more and more people wanted to develop and change it for the better. This is especially true of the great empires that ruled the world - Greek, Persia, even Macedonia, and Rome. The coins had an image of the different gods they had served or emperors who had ruled in to act as a mark of authenticity. (Because even in that time people tried to make fake money! Therefore, it was best to make the coins hard to forge.)

In 118 BC - China started to create leather money. Leather money was made from white deerskin and could be considered as the very first banknote ever. One of these deerskins was as valuable as 40,000 'cash' or a metal coin (Honick, 2021).

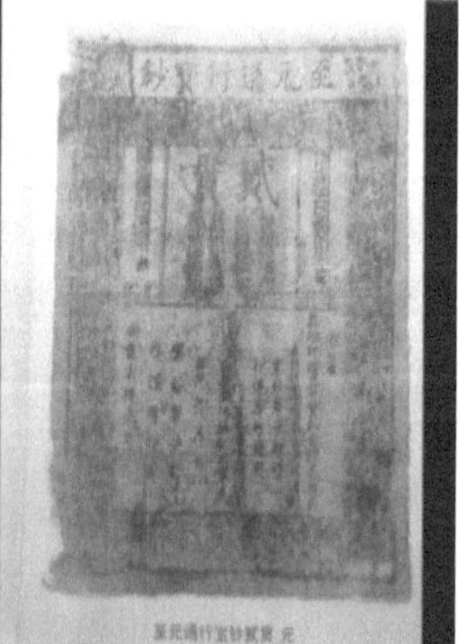

Source: Sutori

The Growth in The Rest of The World

Many areas of Europe still consistently used metal coins as the only means of payments and currencies dating up to the late 16th century. This is because they got possession of many new territories, allowing them to gain constant sources of precious metals - making coins still an easy accessory (Beattie, 2021).

However, lugging around so many coins for far travels was not only impractical but also very unsafe. Banks were created, where they designed paper notes. People could place their money in the bank for exchange of such papers and come back any time to the bank for exchange of metal coins again. Or even the paper money itself could be used to buy certain goods as well as services. It was far more practical and safe. A person had a lot less to carry, and the government was now responsible for the issuing of most currencies.

Currency Wars

Well, history is full of wars, there was even something called a currency war. This is because paper money allowed international trade (buying items all over the world) to start. However, other countries had different forms of currencies. This meant that one currency had a different value over another. Countries would compete, trying to change the value of the enemy's currencies by driving it down or reducing the ability to buy for the other country. This caused certain countries to have to change their currency (Picardo, 2019).

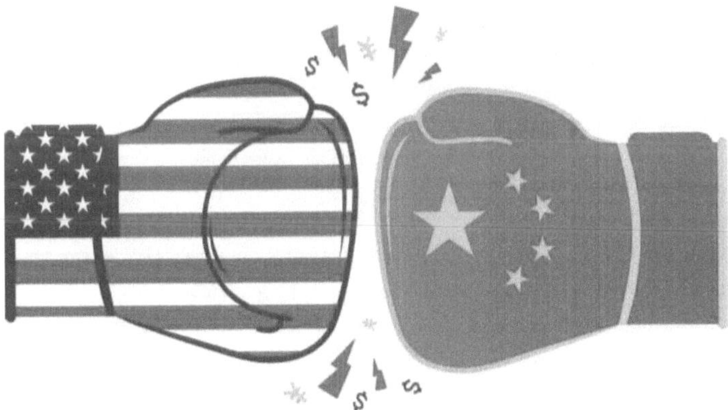

As you may now be aware, not everything can be paid for in dollars. There are still many other currencies in the world. For example, in the UK, there is the pound. In India, it's the rupee, and in South Korea, it's the Won.

How Does Money Work Now?

You probably have worked with cellphones and computers before. Life is becoming more digital, and cash is starting to decrease. Rather, money is starting to change into virtual currency. You can pay for goods and services on your phone for example or even a credit card. So many payments can be done in a virtual way that you do not even have to carry cash around with you to make a payment!

There has even been a creation of digital coins such as Bitcoins, but we will not be diving in too deep, as cryptocurrency should never be considered as a proper form of investment - especially not for children.

At The End of The Day

Money still plays a huge role in this age. Now you know how it started. How it changed, and you know in what forms it can come today. You will likely deal with virtual money rather than real money (unless you are selling items at a flea market). When it comes to investing and investments, most of it is done on a digital basis, and you will have to learn to work with a computer or be assisted by an adult. Keep in mind this very important rule...this rule most people do not follow, but should:

Do not spend any money that you cannot afford to lose. Now, this may be difficult to apply if you don't need to worry too much about money. But this very important rule will save your life in the future. So, remember this line, memorize it, and keep thinking about it as time moves on.

Chapter 3: Earning Money

So is it possible to earn money at this age? Yes! Absolutely! The best part about the day and age you live in is the fact that a computer and internet connection paired with some knowledge is all you need to kick start earning an income. Does it make it easy? No, it comes with hard work and dedication, but by the end of the day, almost anyone is now capable of earning money, regardless of age. And to start learning how to invest, it may be a good idea to earn some extra money.

But before we start with all the ideas, it is best to take one last look at how far money has truly come. We have brushed on the history of money in the previous chapter, but more on a matter of how money was created. Now we will be taking a peek at the timeline:

Timeline of Money

In the Bronze Age of the year 3000 B.C, money was starting to become a commodity. This means that money was created out of objects that had worth. This added to the authenticity as well as a more widespread form of exchange. For example, the use of cowry shells (Beattie, 2021).

China started to make miniature replicas around 1100 B.C where you could design bronze replicas of items that were already of

use. To get a sword, you would need to have a miniature bronze equivalent of a sword to get one. This was, however, quite impractical, because having to carry around so many objects made you a target, added to your burden of travels, and far more likely to get killed for your money (Philosopher's Library, n.d.).

The first official currency that has been recorded was the Lydian Lion around the year 600 B.C. As mentioned before, this is now where modern Turkey now resides. King

Alyattes had the coins minted, and it is the first official currency that has ever been proved. There is a likelihood that there had been currencies before theirs, but so much evidence of history has been lost this will be incredibly hard to discover (Beattie, 2021).

Then in 700 A.D in the Tang Dynasty of China, paper money came into existence. The government had realized the need for lighter loads to perform bigger transactions. However, there was a message on some of them, "If you fake it we will cut your head,"- for anyone who tries to forge them. This is quite a serious threat they gave to criminals.

In the year 1200 A.D, paper notes arrived due to the travels of the incredible explorer Marco Polo. However, until the year 1661, the first Banknote was issued in Sweden (Beattie, 2021).

The US Dollar was then invented in 1792, on April the 2nd. This is when the coins and notes officially came to life in the United States of America. From March 3, 1933, to August 15, 1971, President Franklin D Roosevelt had all the banks in the U.S.A closed. This was because of the run at gold reserves. This was because the banks held a lot of the

gold which was used in the exchange for U.S dollars, and there was a certain fixed exchange rate between the two (Blessing, 2020).

When the president made this bold move, he banned the ability to exchange dollars for gold for a short period. Then he made an order for Americans to turn and exchange the gold they had for U.S dollars. This move allowed Fort Knox to now have the largest supply of gold globally and fully pushed the citizens to use American dollars rather than gold. They also made dollars dependent on currencies rather than gold (Wikipedia contributors, 2021).

In 1946, the first bank card was issued. This was all under a program of "Charge-It" where the idea was a merchant could send the sales slip into the bank and the bank would pay them and charge the customer (Charge It, 2017).

In 1950, Frank McNamara designed a card that could allow you to dine in restaurants, and the Diners club would pay your bill. Afterward, you would repay them later. It was originally designed for a small group of people, but the idea caught on like wildfire, and within a year there were about 20,000 cardholders! (History and Legacy, n.d.)

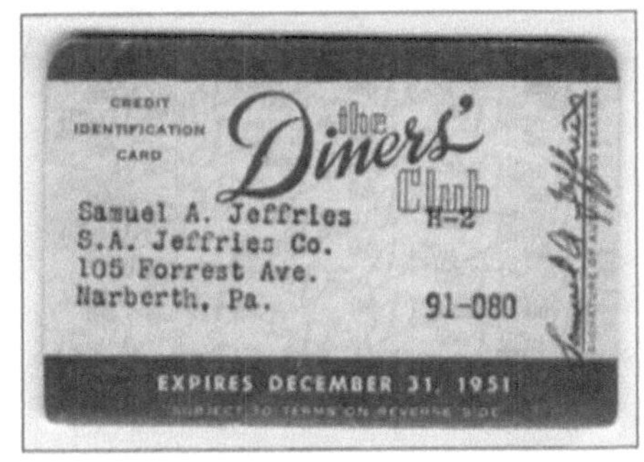

In 1990, PayPal and digital money came to being. PayPal changed the world for the better, allowing you to make payments from a computer to another computer in a matter of seconds. In 2009, Bitcoin and cryptocurrencies had started (Philosopher's Library, n.d.).

How can I Earn Money?

So now that you understand which way the world is heading, it is best to consider digital and physical options in matters of earning some extra cash. After all, it is far safer to stay at home and easier than to set up a lemonade stand outside and hope to sell something in that manner.

Washing Cars

Let us start with an age-old job that can get you some extra cash without much stress. Many people do not have the time to wash their cars as it takes a lot of time and can get very messy. So, there is always a major job opportunity there! A great way to get started is to advertise on social media, or with an adult, go door to door to offer your services. It may seem scary at first, but once you get used to it, you will be doing yourself a major favor! (Bell, 2021)

Becoming an Influencer

If you like being in front of a camera, and your parents don't mind, then this is a classic and great way to start earning money! This takes a lot of time and effort, but in reality, those are two things you have right now. So, keep building your following until  you are officially able to monetize the accounts you have. You do, however, have to be 13 years or older to sign up on most platforms. Even Instagram and Tik Tok are really good ways to build an audience and make some extra cash too (Kultkid, 2019).

Becoming a Streamer

If you are into video games, then streaming is certainly the way to go! This is how adults are making a living - doing something they love? So why not set up and start now? Streamers do make money by selling subscriptions, displaying ads as well as working with brands. All you need to do is build your viewership (Bell, 2021).

Sell Stuff At A Farmers Market

Whether it is your freshly baked chocolate brownies or your beautiful hand-crafted bracelets, take advantage of farmers' markets nearby to start your own little business! You can even grow fruits and veggies to sell or create homemade jams. All these items normally sell well at higher prices (Nationwide, 2021).

Mowing Lawns

An age-old job that still needs doing now and then. It is also an easy and classic way to earn a little extra cash. And this is not even weeding or other forms of gardening! **Offering to cut people's lawns can** help you earn a little extra without too much work! (Carosa, 2021)

Becoming A Video Editor

All you need is one great video editing software and take on some good video editing gigs **online. You don't have to be a movie master pro, and you can take your time building up** more jobs and even possibly a career! Video editors are high in demand after all! (Kate, 2020)

Sell Your Art

If art is something you enjoy and have a talent in, then why not make some money off of it? Selling your work on Etsy or eBay as well as on private platforms is a great way to kickstart this journey (Bell, 2021).

Start A Blog

The reason why this is ideal for you at your age is that you need some time and patience to earn money here. You can earn money from a blog when you have a bigger readership. Then you can do affiliate marketing, sponsored posts, and ads. All these

are a little technical, so ask an adult for help if need be (Bell, 2021).

Now here is a list of plenty more ideas you can certainly consider:

- Taking online surveys
- Creating a YouTube Channel
- Holding a Garage Sale
- Babysit
- Photography
- Selling T-Shirts
- Sell Your Crafts
- Create Games
- Enter into Contests
- Build Websites for Other People
- Cleaning Service
- Run Errands
- Setup of Social Media Accounts
- Organize Closets
- Shoe Shining
- Carpet Cleaning
- Window Washing
- Selling Gold Balls - collecting them on golf courses that had been lost. Clean them and resell

***Take note:**

There are other job opportunities such as pet sitting or dog walking, but the reason why this was not mentioned is because of the danger posed when dealing with other people's animals. Although the majority of animals are well trained. Depending on your age and your experience it is best to take on jobs with animals if you are confident, secure, and have a greater understanding of how to deal with difficult pets. Again, many of these jobs listed have their risks, but with pets, it can be unpredictable. Be sure that your parents are aware of each job you want to take on. If they can get involved and help you out it would be even better!

As you can see, there are plenty of jobs available for anyone who has the work ethic and set their minds to it! You can do it!

Chapter 4: Banking

Where do people normally store their money? Well, if you answered a bank. That would be correct. After all, money is safer behind a vault and security guards than under a pillow in your house. The banks also make it easy to make payments for shopping with the use of credit cards, and even now mobile apps that simply scan and pay. To use those tools, you will need a bank account. That is why it is best to know what you can do about it.

History of Banking

So, this poses the question, where did banking start? Banks have been around for a while now, but they share important history for you to know and understand. Banking has been existing since the first currencies were truly minted. The currency was commonly in coins, created for taxation. When empires started growing, there had to be a system where people could pay and distribute wealth.

Banking began when empires needed a form or method to make payments for foreign services or goods with items that could very easily be exchanged. Coins varied in size, but eventually, they got replaced by fragile paper.

But before paper bills were designed, the coins needed safe storage space. Houses were so insecure, and coins weighed a lot. It was impractical to travel around with the money, and ancient homes  could not keep their wealth safe in vaults. In the Roman era, the wealthy people resorted to storing their goods under the basements of temples. Because the temples were filled with priests as well as temple workers, there was a natural assumption to their honesty, and that their belongings were safe (Beattie, 2021).

There are even records of Egypt, Rome, Greece, and Babylon that had temples that loan money out (Wikipedia contributors, 2021). This means people in ancient times had debts with the temples! Temples worked a little like a bank for many of the cities. This is why they were the first to be attacked when people stormed a city.

Coins were a lot easier to hoard because of their small size, and merchants even took to borrowing and repaying with interest to those who were desperately in need. Temples were the places that handled bigger loans for people, even sovereigns.

So Where Was the First Official Bank?

Would it surprise you if you knew it was in Rome? The Romans were good at building and paperwork. Most spending, loaning, and borrowing occurred at an institutional bank there. Julius Caesar had changed a law, allowing banks to take land if the people who owed money could not pay it back in time. This caused a massive shift in the power banks had over people as well as the noblemen because many of them had massive debts that they just passed on to their descendants unless of course, the lineage died out (Beattie, 2021).

However, the Roman Empire did come to an end - but many of the banking institutions survived - normally in the form of papal bankers from the Roman Empire as well as the Knights of Templar. Some people acted as small-time moneylenders. They tended to compete against the church.

Visa Royal

Many of the monarchs became aware of the power that lay within the banking institutions. The banks that existed had many loans taken out by people who ruled. This caused hard times to the treasury because the king could make extravagant purchases without much need to pay the banks back.

It had come to such a point that in 1557, King Phillip II from Spain had created so much debt in his country - that he caused the world's first national form of bankruptcy, then the second, then the third, then fourth at a rapid pace (Koenigsberger).

Modern Banking

Banking was already existing within the British Empire when a man by the name of Adam Smith worked to limit the state's power and involvement in a bank. This opened the world to capitalism-which is allowing businesses to grow and expand without the government getting involved.

At first, though, Adam's idea did not seem to help. An average bank may just have survived for five years, but Alexander Hamilton created a system that worked to keep banks afloat, he created a liquid market and pushed out the competition that was not legal (Wikipedia contributors, 2021).

Because many of the other banks had not been legal when this system was established, there was a great level of mistrust people had for them.

Merchant Banks

Many of the duties within an economy were to be handled by that of a national banking system. This meant that loans and business finance were normally controlled by merchant banks. They used their connections to build political as well as financial power.

In the year 1907, a collapse in business shares caused many people to panic. They stormed into banks trying to sell their stock. This caused a huge knock on the value of the shares of the business. J.P. Morgan took control to stop the panic and cause people to calm down (The Investopedia Team, 2021).

In 1929, the trade slowed down, and there was a stock market crash (where the value of many businesses and investments failed). It was called a Black Tuesday because many people lost their money as well as their jobs. This in turn caused a disaster for the country overall, and all banks had to face massive consequences. After this, there were very clear rules set out for banks (Wikipedia, 2021).

Banks were given rules to follow for the people to trust in them, but no one believed them, and the area remained in depression (when there are greater expenses than income flowing through a city).

However, World War II played a part in the recovery of the country and saved banks from being obliterated. The war needed billions of dollars to carry on, and many companies decided to build huge credit with them, and eventually turn into a global market. Finally, the countries started to settle. The trust between banks grew, and an average person had good access to insurance, mortgages, and other forms of credit-credit means of borrowing money (Goodwin, 2021).

Knowing about the banks, in general, isn't enough to proceed. There is much more to know and understand about the banks and how they work. Whenever you need to connect your finances with any bank, you need to have an account there. A bank account is an account that the bank maintains to save and transact your finances. Banks or other financial institutions keep the records of your financial transaction through your bank accounts (Wikipedia).

Types of Accounts

Now chances are your parents both own a bank account. You may or may not already have one yourself, but have you ever wondered why there are different account names? Well, let's take a look at the different bank accounts you can indeed open.

Current Account

This is known as a deposit account for traders, entrepreneurs, business owners, and people who need to both make as well as receive payments on a more regular basis. This means the money tends to come and go quickly, flowing to and fro (thus called liquid). There is no limit to the number of transactions you can make in a day, and you cannot earn any form of interest with this account.

Savings Account

This works like a deposit account. You place money and you earn some interest (a small amount of money gets paid into your account over a certain period). The number of transactions you can make on this account are limited and there are different kinds of savings accounts. Some offer higher interest (more payments received every month), but that normally means you need to give a greater warning when you want to withdraw money from your account. A savings account can be opened for children, women, seniors, families, and more.

Salary Account

This is an account that is connected to you, your employer, and the bank. Because you are not likely to have a job at this time, this account is not too important to know about. However, just so you know, this bank account is used to have your monthly salary paid in if you do have a job.

Fixed Deposit Account

This is where you have an account where you receive a fixed amount of interest (payment) every month or every three months. However, this does mean you need to pay a certain amount of money to open an account like this, and you have to wait before you can withdraw money.

Checking Accounts

A checking account is used to deposit the payment and keep daily spending records. This account comes with checks and a debit card. You can use these checks and cards to spend the money that is not in your account actually.

Investment and Retirement Accounts

When you need to open an account in a bank, you can ask for an investment account. This will be a brokerage account for your investments. You can use it to invest your money in bonds, mutual funds, bonds, and other financial items.

(Nova Credit, 2020)

Chapter 5: Safety While Earning

If you have worked on the internet before, you are probably familiar with viruses'. But considering that your plan is to invest online, what does that mean for you? It means that you have to take extra steps to stay safe! You may not be able to see the risks or dangers (considering they are hidden in a line of code), but you need to be aware that there are some things you need to be careful of while working online - especially when there is money involved.

Consider the internet is one big marketplace. In the marketplace, you can find all sorts of goodies and items to buy and sell. But in between, there are a couple of people trying to sell you duds or literally just steal your money from you. There are others who already

try to destroy and corrupt what you already have. There are many pickpockets, trying to steal your information and use it to either sell or get more money from you (Safe Search Kid, 2021).

This is how the internet works, and this is why you need to follow certain rules in order to avoid the bad guys on the internet. Although this does not make you completely bulletproof, you will be good at handling 90% of the worst and common criminals on the internet out there. Now isn't that just neat? This is because the people on the internet target the gullible and the people desperate to make money. They love to sweet talk people into giving their information. Don't fall for this trap!

Top Rules to Stay Safe Online

The following are the rules to implement when you decide to work online. These rules help you to stay safe from scams and online fraud.

Keep the Information You Share Limited

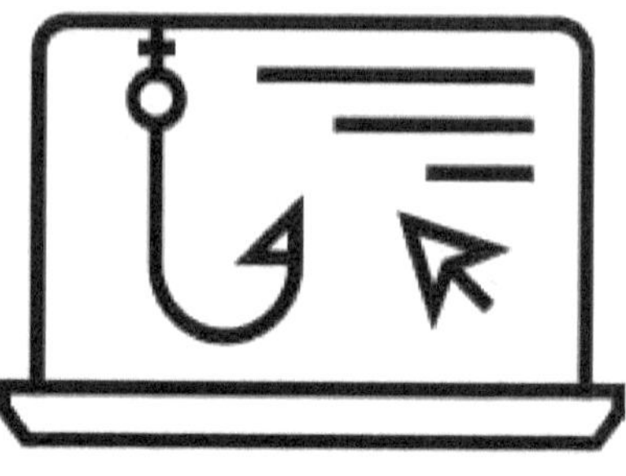

Personal information should be limited at least and avoided at most. Most employers and customers online do not need to know where you live, as well as altogether your bank account details (unless you are making a purchase on the website - if so, make sure it is a safe website). When it comes to your life online, do not hand out any unnecessary personal information about yourself publically either - especially on social media. There is such a thing as an online stalker, and this is where they can get most of the information from you (Safe Search Kid, 2021).

Consider this, you won't be handing out your credit card or street address or even your last name on the street. So why would you want to do that to millions of people who are online?

Keeping the Privacy Settings, You Have On

People in the marketplace want to know as much information about you as they can, but here is the problem, so do the hackers. And you can give them a backdoor where you browse and the social media that you use. But it can also be up to you to take control of your information. The people can't take what you don't upload, or if you close the backdoor with some steel bars. Try either on your own or with an adult to boost the privacy settings on all the software and apps that you use. Even Facebook has very specialized settings for you to use, making it hard for companies and hackers to actually discover your personal information.

Being A Safe browser

Google cannot filter every bad website and considering you would not normally walk in a bad neighborhood, don't browse in a bad online neighborhood. Cybercriminals love to use clickbait as well as different forms of content to lure you in. The problem is, if you click onto one bad website, you can let malware in. So, it is best to have your anti-virus set up to scan the website before even entering and be very careful of suggested links. Even if you visit a safe website, sometimes ads are placed to lead you to a bad one.

A Great Way to Play It Safe, Use a VPN

So, what on earth is a VPN? Well, let's start with an IP address. The IP Address is basically your digital signal that you give whenever you are visiting various kinds of websites, you are leaving your IP address, indicating to the websites where you are.

Now, this can be tracked, and although it is mostly harmless, you want to keep the cybercriminals away from you. This is where VPN comes in. VPN hides your IP Address and keeps you from being tracked or traced. This makes using the websites infinitely safer, and this is especially important at your age.

Be Very Careful of What You Download

The main goal of bad people on the internet is tricking you into downloading something onto your computer. Normally this gives easy and direct access for viruses and malware to infect your computer to either steal or corrupt information. It may all look well and innocent, but if you are not 100% completely sure what you are downloading is safe then you need to take a step back and reconsider what you are doing.

Choose Strong Passwords

It is easy to choose passwords that you can remember, but they tend to be easy as well as weak. It is up to you to choose strong passwords, despite it taking longer and being tougher to remember. Strong passwords keep people from breaking in easily. In fact, it can prevent many hackers from attempting to get inside.

Keep the Antivirus Up to Date

New viruses are constantly being made, and this is why you need to constantly keep your antivirus up to date. This is because antivirus is doing its best to keep up, combating viruses and identifying malware to keep your computers safe. Therefore the best plan of action is to keep it updated.

So these steps are all good and well, but what do you do to avoid possible investment scams? This is where you have to filter through the different investment choices and be able to choose from the options. There is always the risk of choosing the wrong one and losing your money. There are certain steps you can take (Safe Search Kid, 2021).

Avoiding Investment Scams

First, don't be scared to ask questions. Most con artists say that you won't investigate before you give the money. However, do not just ask the questions to them, find out information from other sources, and take your time to do more forms of your own research. People are very verbal on the web, and the likelihood that you are the first one

to be scammed is very small. So it is very easy to discover scams if you just ask the right questions.

Any investments you need to make are worthy of a decent amount of research. Looking into different financial statements or having an adult look into it is always a good idea. The less information you can find about a company, the more suspicious it can truly become (Fowler, 2021).

Know your salesperson - you need to spend some time getting to know the person offering the investments. Even if you have known them a little while beforehand, you want to make sure they are actually licensed to sell the specific securities in the states, and you can even check the disciplinary history of brokers and advisers completely free on the FINRA's and SEC's databases. (These are databases making sure all the public information is readily available for everyone to get access to.)

Be very careful of offers that were not solicited (basically they approached you - you did not approach them). Even if they have been praised online but do not offer the proper financial information from different/dependant sources. This could be something known as the "pump and dump" scheme, where something is bound to go wrong, and it is near impossible to track your money down.

Familiarize yourself and your family members with all the various kinds of fraud that come with investments. The more you know about the different types of frauds, the more easily you'll be able to spot them when they come your way.

Be careful as well of the following persuasion tactics commonly used to convince you into making the wrong investment:

- *If it sounds way too good to be true, then it is.* This is because riches are promised for investments that do not provide enough information on how it will go. Besides, all investments have risks. To promise otherwise is plain foolish or it is a scam. People take the risk away to help people invest - when in reality, investing in someone or business that makes promises such as these are the biggest risks after all.
- *Guaranteed returns are not a thing* - but scammers and con artists love to make such promises. As mentioned above, each investment has too much risk. If they try to plant images in your head of someone who is rich, be very careful. They like to play on the desperate.
- *Everyone is busy buying it* - again, another massive scam. This is because they try to create FOMO (fear of missing out). However, if you tackle that statement, you will find it crumbling to the ground. This is just a tactic used to get people to invest as quickly as possible.
- *Reciprocity* - fraudsters even do their best to lure people in by inviting them to free seminars or webinars. It works for them doing a small favor for you, in return, you can do a massive favor for them. So always make sure you

- know that the product is right for you, understand exactly what you are buying as well as any and all associated fees that actually come with this.

(*Investment Fraud Attorneys, n.d.*)

Verifying

The best step to root out fraudsters is by verifying the information that is sent to you. For example, the most basic method is by going directly to the source and calling people. Especially when it comes to news about people and more that is posted on social media.

Second, it is always best to rely on first-hand witnesses. So, if you can discover anybody who has invested in a certain product or business - it would be ideal to have a conversation with them first if at all possible.

When checking things out on social media, check out the credibility of a person. Be very careful of brand-new accounts. This is because many scammers are rooted out quickly, their accounts blocked, and therefore are in constant need to make new accounts. Check out a person's friends and followers, is the account used on a regular basis?

When you are verifying website information, you can check with WHOIS lookup, in order to check who really registered the URL. This will allow you to access the internet archive and get a good idea of the person and whether or not the information they give is credible (*Common Scams and Frauds | USAGov, n.d.*).

Next, you can even verify images, such as checking out the language, license plates, signs, languages, etc. You can also check out TinEye which allows you to see where an image had actually come from - basically, whether it was copy-pasted (a good tactic also to discover whether or not you are being catfished).

And there you have it! Caution to stay safe while investing, tactics to verify the information, and general ideas on how to avoid getting scammed. When you are learning how to earn and invest, you must learn about budgeting and how to manage your income. If you follow most of these steps, you are already one step ahead of the average investor. And you are still so young!

Chapter 6: Budgeting - Learn How to Handle Your Income

So what happens when you start earning money? What do you do then? Well, there is a very important step to learn in the world of finances and investing. And do you want to know a big secret? Most people don't practice this step as they should. As a matter of fact, many of them don't even know how to do this! Do you have a guess?

If you said backflips. You are correct, but there is also budgeting. What on earth is budgeting? It is basically a plan you set up with your money to make sure you spend and save the right amounts. Most people do not budget as they should.

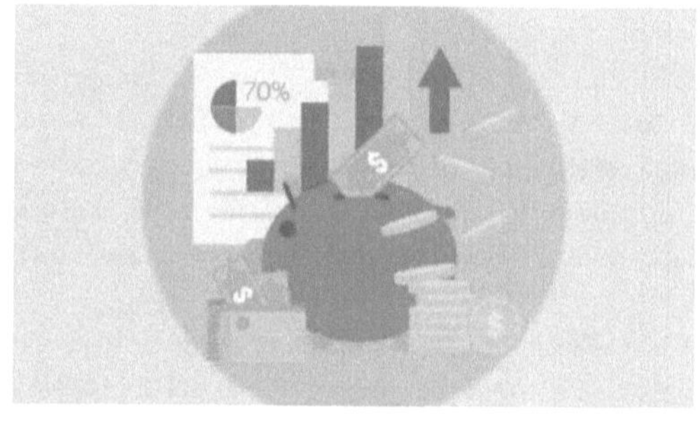

If you learn the secrets of budgeting at a young age, you will be doing yourself a massive favor. This is because this well-crafted skill will keep your money in check, allowing you **to make sure you don't** overspend on any items, and the money actually goes where it needs to go. So here are some steps on how to budget properly - and the faster you learn this, the better! (Bruce, 2021)

Basics of Budgeting

Now remember the following, budgeting is actually a living thing. This is because it is constantly moving, having expenses, income, and everything to keep track of. Your budget will also always be changing as your life changes. Expecting it to remain exactly the same is basically saying nothing will be changing in your life either. But you already know that what happened at the beginning of this year and what will be happening at the end is very different. So here is a step-by-step guide of what you need to do to set up a budget.

Note the amount of income coming in

First, start off by making an estimate of the amount of money you have coming in on a monthly or weekly basis. Rather underestimate than overestimate, and make sure you write this number down.

Track the spending that you do

Keep track of any purchases you are making. If you don't know how much you are spending, how can you possibly plan and keep track of it in the long haul? It would also be a lot easier to see where you are overspending, and where you can actually start cutting costs.

Set The Goals

Want to save up for an Xbox game? Or do you want to buy a camera? Set goals! How much money you want to earn, how much money you want to spend, and how much money you want to save. Goals can help you form a plan which is the next step.

Making a Plan

With all the expenses and income, you have tracked, now it is time to set up a plan for the following few months. Write down how much you should make as well as how much you are going to spend - break your expenses down into different categories. Even your savings will count in this budget, as you want to make sure every penny you have is spoken for.

Adjustments

Once you have tried out your first budget, you will come to pick up on any changes that may need to be made. Spent too much on popcorn? Cut the costs and place the money over into savings for the car. Skip a movie night in order to make sure you can spend money for your outing with your friends the next day. All these will help you pick and choose - a very important skill to learn when it comes to budgeting, life, and finances in general.

Never Stop Checking in

Make sure you are always keeping proper track of your finances. Make sure you know that you are staying on par and learn to adjust if you happen to overspend. At the end of the day, you want to learn the habit of keeping track of your expenses and sticking to the plan. This is by far the biggest favor you can truly do for yourself as you start growing up and have to face the financial predicaments later in life.

But this may beg the question, why is budgeting so important? Why is it necessary to help your financial journey? Well, here are a few good reasons why you need to budget (Schwab Brokerage).

Why Should You Budget?

Firstly, the budget will really help you to get good control of your finances. Just because you earn money does not mean you actually have control of it. You will find your older self, thanking you left right and center for mastering this skill. Just because it really can hinder or destroy your success if you do not know this skill.

Secondly, being able to budget allows you to achieve any goals you may have. Whether it is your college funds or your vacation, or your latest cell phone. Being able to budget allows you to set money aside for things that you want even though they may be more expensive. All you need is the proper time and patience for it (Khan, 2017).

Thirdly, budgeting will really help to keep you honest. If you keep a good track record of your money and what you are spending it on, it can keep you accountable to reach your goals. If you keep a good budget, then you have to keep track of every single coin you spent on. This is a good, as well as a powerful motivator to keep your spending on track, allowing you to reach your goals faster.

Budgeting can also help improve bad habits or reduce the chances of you getting one. If you learn how to budget at a very early age, then you are doing yourself a massive favor. This is because you will not learn many bad habits that people who do not budget learn.

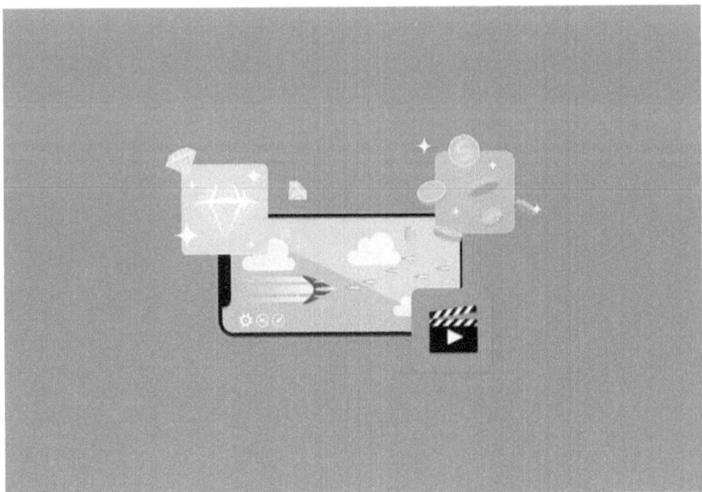

It teaches you self-control, a very important trait to be successful in everyday life (Schwab Brokerage).

Finally, budgeting can really help you to avoid debt or help you get rid of debt as quickly as possible. It is never nice to owe someone money, so good budgeting can help you avoid it or help you get rid of it so much quicker. Now is that not neat?

So, in the world of budgeting, you have now seen the steps you can take and why you should take it. Especially at your age, there is not a lot to keep track of, so it puts you a step ahead. Budgeting will be easier, and by the time it starts to get more complicated, you will have such a good habit of when to spend and when to save that it can hardly be called a challenge.

Chapter 7: When to Spend and When to Save

In line with budgeting, you may be good at planning, but how can you stick to the plan? This is by learning the balance of spending and saving. This can be a tough and tricky habit to adopt, and I am here to help! Just like learning how to mine, you need a few tricks in order to find the golden nugget faster.

The Art of Self-Control

Why does self-control really matter? Well, it is a form of willpower, it is having the ability to control yourself, your actions, and even your thoughts in order to get a better outcome. How many times do you remember people getting angry at you, and things just get worse from there on? This is because the person lacked the self-control necessary in order to really practice patience despite getting really mad. This is self-control, and it is a very important aspect of people's lives.

Self-control can also help you to eliminate distractions, do better at school, and even get to your chores. It means you are less inclined to get in trouble and do better. And when it comes to budgeting, it makes life a whole lot easier. If you are trying to invest, and work on earning money, then the need for self-control is equally critical (Team Understood, 2021).

So here are a couple of steps you can learn to practice a little more self-control. Consider adding it to your everyday life, surprise your friends and family members!

Out of Sight - Out of Mind

When it comes to anything that can distract you during your work and school and finances, keep it out of sight! If your phone keeps you away from your budgeting, ask your mother to keep it for you until you are done with your budgeting (present the proof). If you have the habit of playing video games right after school, pack it away and only bring it out once you have completed all your homework. Little tips like that can truly make all the difference in the world (*Thinking Skills: Focus*, 2017).

Reward Yourself for Work Accomplished

Why not buy yourself a bag of candy to reward yourself whenever you get something done? Or it is even better if your parents can set up a system for you. Treat yourself to a chocolate or a toy whenever you get a certain amount of money, or to a candy whenever you clean your room (Good Character, 2020).

Set Yourself Reminders

The best way to get something done is to remind yourself to do it. Set up on your phone or calendar all the tasks you need to get done and remember to do it! It is very easy to lose track of all the matters and items in life. But with a daily if not an hourly reminder, you can get everything you need done.

Allow Yourself to Take a Break

Teatime breaks, lunchtime breaks, and even afternoon breaks are all needed. Allow yourself time to play, have fun, go out with friends, and still experience parts of your childhood. You are allowed to have your fun. You are allowed to take a break. If not, life can become dull and dreary. This is why many adults themselves can become incredibly bored of their work. It is because they do not have any room to have a little bit of fun and joy in their life.

Turn the Tasks of "Must Do" into a "Want To"

This is where you need to decide that you want to do your tasks instead of needing to. It is a mindset that you need to adopt. For example, instead of thinking, I must do the dishes - you should say I want to do the dishes. It may seem too simple or too easy. But sometimes the too simple and too easy solutions are what gets the tasks done after all.

Practice Planning

Take each and every day as a new opportunity to practice your ability to plan and stick to it. This means that each day you can work on practicing your self-control. After all, if you are familiar with sports or drawing, you will have to practice each and every day. The same can be said for planning. In order to get better at planning, you need practice after all (Sippl, 2021).

Finally, when you think you have learned a lot about money, how to earn and spend it, it is time to jump into the field of investing. Get your parents or adults involved in your decisions. When you decide to invest, let them help you stay on track and keep focused. After all, they can keep you accountable, and help practice your planning,  budgeting, and spending. It may seem dreadful at first, but in reality, it would be very helpful throughout the investing process.

Chapter 8: Investing Money

Investing is one of the wisest, most productive methods at earning money. This is known as a passive form of income. What does it mean to be passive? Well, very little work is put into it, but you will still receive money! Now, this may seem a little too good to be true. Well, it can be - if you are not careful. This is why it is time to take a peek at investments to understand everything you need to know. For example, when starting with an investment, a lot of work needs to be done before being able to just let the money grow.

Introduction To Investing

Investing is always changing. That is why it is best to jump on the bus as early as possible and learn to stay up to date. But there are a couple of basic principles that once you undertake them, you should have a foundational knowledge of investing. As there are some core principles which can help you succeed in earning money, even at your age!

Investing is placing money into a business, asset, or another potential item in hopes of getting a return (profit from the money that was initially placed).

First, investments are made of a risk ladder. This means, depending on where you are in investing, there are higher risks and lower risks. What are the risks I am referring to? Well, sometimes you spend money, but then you do not get anything in return. Some investments have a bigger chance of you losing money in comparison to others (Picardo, 2021).

But here is one big rule in investing: there can never be a 100% guarantee of making a profit. If anyone tells you that an investment will always pay off, be very careful. No true investment works this way, and you may be falling into a scam.

Different Types of Investment

Now, the simplest and safest investment form is a cash bank deposit. They are by far the easiest, simplest forms of investing and safest too. Because you will have a greater understanding of what you will be receiving.

However, this form of investing does not normally beat inflation. *What is inflation?* Have you ever realized how items become more expensive as time passes by? Well, this is inflation, and the value of $100 gradually becomes less and less as time passes by. So to 'keep' the value of the $100, you will have to earn the same amount of money as inflation rises. But when it comes to cash bank deposits, you do not normally earn enough - which means you might still be losing money.

Bonds

Bonds are a form of debt that is created between the investor and the person who is borrowing. You will be lending out money to someone, and they will be paying you back over time with interest. Naturally, the interest you receive will be the profit of your investment. You can normally buy bonds from corporations or a government agency and is a very common form of financing for businesses.

The amount of interest you earn depends on the interest rate (percentage) and so people tend to invest in bonds when interest rates happen to be rising in banks etc.

How can I make money with this? While you are busy lending the money, the person borrowing it will be paying interest. Depending on how old the bond is and when the money is returned, depends on how much money you make. Naturally the longer the money is borrowed, the more interest, and therefore more profit (Dragon, 2021).

Stocks

This is likely to be the kind of investing that you will be focusing on for now. Stocks are small parts of ownership for a business. The business then pays you with their profits for owning a part of their business. This is normally called a dividend. The amount of dividend you get depends on the number of stocks you have as well as how much profit the business has made. The harsh truth is that if the business struggles to make money for a certain period, then you are not likely to receive a dividend. So you have to be very careful with the business you happen to choose.

How can I make money here? Well, you will buy stock (normally with the help of an adult) - remember to do some research on the business first. Ask yourself - is the business doing well? How old is it? What are people saying about this business? The older, more established the business is with a history of making a profit, the better. Once you have purchased stocks, you can either wait for the value of the stock to rise and resell it. Then you make money from the extra cash you have received, or you can wait and receive dividends. Tip: if you see the value of the stock sinking over a certain period, it is best to sell your stock to make sure you do not have a big loss (Adams, 2021).

Mutual Funds

This is when you place money into one singular fund. But this fund happens to buy up a variety of different stocks. Then split up the dividends and share this with you. You can either manage this yourself or have others manage it for you. The advantage of this is that you spread your risk. It means that if one business were to fail, you can still make a profit from the other profits that are succeeding (Thune, 2021).

How can I make money?

Buy into the fund from a managing firm or discount brokerage. It would be recommended to consider a managing firm at this point as you are still building up experience. Oftentimes with discount brokerages, you need to tell them what to buy whereas the firms buy into companies based on their experiences and knowledge. Take a look at what businesses they invest in and learn why they made those decisions. You can learn a lot while making money. Which is a bonus!

Commodities

This is a pirate's treasure, where you buy gold, silver, or any number of items in this world that are valuable. Then you wait for the best value of the silver or gold which you have purchased and resell it for a profit (*What Are Commodity Funds?*, n.d.).

Now there are many other options for investing, but at this point and time, you are not likely to be able to afford these kinds of investing:

- *Real estate investing* - this is when you purchase a house and rent it out
- *Hedge funds and private equity funds* - this is when you invest in a large variety of assets which can cost up to $1 million or even higher and can take a long time before you can receive the money again
- *Cryptocurrencies* - this has a lot of potential in making money, but without experience and an in-depth understanding of how crypto works, you can get yourself into big trouble. It is too high of a risk to consider as a good form of investment. People have to invest in this at their own risk and is not recommended here - especially at your age (James Royal, Ph.D., 2021).

Top Tips when Making An Investment

You can't always walk into a building and tell the people there you want to invest. And depending on your age, you may also not necessarily be at the right age. This is where your parents or a grown adult can help you. Once you have made enough money and you want to start investing, you will need to complete a couple of steps:

1. *Choose where you are going to invest* - you want to know where you are going to invest - such as bonds, or banks, or mutual funds. Once you understand that you can move on to the next step (Coombes, 2021).

2. *Do your research.* You want to know everything you can about the businesses you are interested in. If you struggle to understand what is going on, ask an adult, if they even struggle, don't consider investing in that business.

3. *Get more information* - The less information you can find out about the area you want to invest in, the riskier the investment. Preferably you want to invest in a completely transparent organization - most information is easy to get a hold of then (Coombes, 2021).

4. *Find a good broker* - brokers are people who normally purchase the shares for you. You can either get a full-service broker, but they will be more expensive and more inclined for people who are investing full time (they do help to build a financial plan as well as keep you informed on the most potential investments), or you can get a discount broker. Then, you or your parents will tell them what to do, buy and sell in return for a small commission fee (familyeducation.com, 2017).

5. *Invest!* When you have found a trustworthy broker, it is time to invest.

6. *Wait and keep an eye on it.* If you see things are going well, leave the investment there, but if you see that the value of the investment is reducing, try to cut costs by selling it as soon as possible. However, ask for advice on this matter. Because some investments may sink in value only to bounce back and make a profit later.

There you have it! This is how you can start placing your money and watching it grow! Suddenly it does not seem so hard or complicated after all. However, it is again recommended to have an adult help you with these decisions because many of them have a better experience. However, remember to do your research, and that the decision should ultimately be in your hands.

Leave a 1-click review!

~

I would be incredibly grateful if you take just 60 seconds to write just a brief review on Amazon, even if it's just a few sentences.

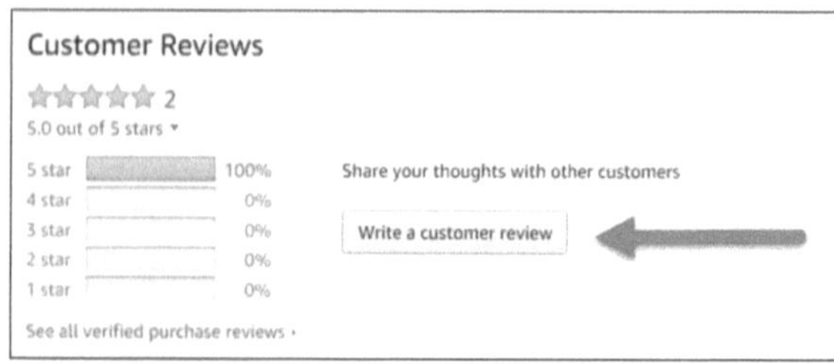

https://www.amazon.com/review/create-review-asin=B09MLBKYFS

Conclusion

Here we are at the end of our tale. You have now mined for some golden nuggets, and you have the information to do so! Be patient and kind with yourself, as it will not be an easy journey. It never is with investing, but it doesn't mean it can't be fun!

Remember, the primary responsibility of the breadwinner is to the parents and adults in your life. What you want to do now is learn how to earn money without having to rush into it like grown-ups do. This is the fun part of being a child, is using your time to earn a little extra money without all the necessary stresses and more!

Furthermore, any help you may need or have should be left to an adult. Struggling to open a bank account? Have an adult help you! Want someone to keep you responsible for all the budgeting and checking on your investments? Adults can help you too! Now it may seem quite dreary from time to time, but in reality, making money is very rewarding -opening doors in which you can indeed participate in either buying fun stuff or actually going on an adventure! Furthermore, there is nothing quite so satisfying as learning skills that most adults don't even practice! This will make you far wiser than the average person!

Also remember, planning is key, without a good plan, how on earth are you supposed to move forward? But a good plan only comes with practice and making sure you stick with the plan can yet again come with repetition. Make plans and learn how to stick to them every single day. Soon you won't be running late for anything, your homework will be on par, and you still should have free time to enjoy yourself as well as make some money. After all, your schedule should not be close to adults.

Remember, finally, to have fun but also to stay safe! The internet is crowded with bad people, so you have to be smart about your approach, otherwise again it can get you into trouble. Make sure whatever computer that you use has the anti-virus and proper equipment to keep your information safe. After all, you don't want anyone stealing your hard work.

And finally, we reach the end of the mine. It has been a long day, but certainly worth it! Don't be afraid to go back and review where necessary. After all, it is quite easy to forget stuff and facts much like the dates in the history lesson. If you are good with remembering those, then well done! Because most people are terrible with dates.

And thus, we now have to bid farewell. It has been such an amazing journey to walk with you, teaching all kinds of wonderful and practical matters in investing. I hope you have learned a lot and see you in the world of finances!

Reviews are a great way for both adults and kids alike to discover new books to read in the future. So, if you enjoyed this book and would recommend it to others, please leave a review on Amazon! Talk about your favorite element of the book and who would enjoy reading it.

Thank you!

My other books you will love!

Amazon.com/dp/B09ML95Q6N

Amazon.com/dp/B09ML9VJCF

Don't forget to grab your GIFT!!!

http://daphnemcooper.com/parenting.pdf

Joining the PME Community

Looking to meet other parents that can help you on your parenting journey? If so, then check out the Parenting Made Easy (PME) Community here:

https://www.facebook.com/groups/293830159257919/

References

A.K. (2021, January 15). *Benefits of Being Financially Stable*. Child Abuse Prevention, Treatment & Welfare Services | Children's Bureau. Retrieved November 10, 2021, from https://www.all4kids.org/news/blog/benefits-of-being-financially-stable/

Adams, R. C. (2021, October 17). *12 Stocks for Kids: Kid-Friendly Stocks to Begin Investing [2021]*. Young and the Invested. Retrieved November 13, 2021, from https://youngandtheinvested.com/stocks-for-kids/

Anderson, K. (2021, April 1). *Guide to the Barter Economy & the Barter System History*. MintLife Blog. https://mint.intuit.com/blog/personal-finance/guide-to-the-barter-economy-the-barter-system-history/

Bank Panic of 1907 Definition. (2021, September 28). Investopedia. Retrieved November 10, 2021, from https://www.investopedia.com/terms/b/bank-panic-of-1907.asp

(Barnum, Forbes). https://www.forbes.com/quotes/7311/

Beattie, A. B. (2021, August 23). *The History of Money: From Barter to Banknotes*. Investopedia. Retrieved November 11, 2021, from https://www.investopedia.com/articles/07/roots_of_money.asp

Beattie, A. B. (2021, May 29). *The Evolution of Banking Over Time*. Investopedia. Retrieved November 11, 2021, from https://www.investopedia.com/articles/07/banking.asp

Bell, S. B. (2021, August 13). *How to Make Money as a Kid*. Money under 30. Retrieved November 10, 2021, from https://www.moneyunder30.com/how-to-make-money-as-a-kid

Blessing, E. B. (2020, December 16). *The Coinage Act of 1792*. Investopedia. Retrieved November 12, 2021, from https://www.investopedia.com/terms/c/the-coinage-act-of-1972.asp

Booth, B. (2020, January 31). *It's not just about saving. Teach your teen to invest now to set them up for a financially healthy life*. CNBC. Retrieved November 10, 2021, from https://www.cnbc.com/2020/01/29/teaching-teenagers-to-invest-now-will-set-them-up-for-life.html

Bruce, K. (2021, May 14). *Budgeting for Kids: How to Teach Budgeting From Age 3 to 18*. Freedom Sprout.Retrieved November 12, 2021, from https://freedomsprout.com/budgeting-for-kids/

Budgeting. (n.d.). Schwab Brokerage. Retrieved November 12, 2021, from https://www.schwabmoneywise.com/teaching-kids/budgeting

Carosa, C. (2021, July 26). *Yes, Babysitting And Lawn Mowing Money Can Go Into A Child IRA*. Forbes. Retrieved November 8, 2021, from https://www.forbes.com/sites/chriscarosa/2021/07/25/yes-babysitting-and-lawn-mowing-money-can-go-into-a-child-ira/

Carlson, B. (2021, October 6). *An Unhealthy Obsession with Money*. Https://Awealthofcommonsense.Com/2021/10/an-Unhealthy-Obsession-with-Money/. Retrieved November 8, 2021, from https://awealthofcommonsense.com/2021/10/an-unhealthy-obsession-with-money/

Charge It. (2017, August 7). National Museum of American History. Retrieved November 11, 2021, from https://americanhistory.si.edu/american-enterprise-exhibition/consumer-era/charge-it

Common Scams and Frauds | USAGov. (n.d.). USA Government. Retrieved November 12, 2021, from https://www.usa.gov/common-scams-frauds

Coombes, A. (2021, February 10). *What to Invest In: Choosing Your Investments.* NerdWallet. Retrieved November 13, 2021, from https://www.nerdwallet.com/article/investing/what-to-invest-in

Corporate Finance Institute. (2021, February 2). *Bartering.* Retrieved November 7, 2021, from https://corporatefinanceinstitute.com/resources/knowledge/economics/bartering/

DeNicola, L. D. N. (2020, July 9). *A guide to the different types of bank accounts in the United States.* Nova Credit. Retrieved November 10, 2021, from https://www.novacredit.com/resources/a-guide-to-the-different-types-of-bank-accounts-in-the-united-states/

Dragon, D. (2021, September 11). *What Bonds Should You Buy for Your Kids?* MyBankTracker. Retrieved November 13, 2021, from https://www.mybanktracker.com/savings/faq/buying-savings-bonds-kids-115764

Dunn, E., & Courtney, C. C. (2021, October 11). *Does More Money Really Make Us More Happy?* Harvard Business Review. Retrieved November 7, 2021, from https://hbr.org/2020/09/does-more-money-really-makes-us-more-happy

Familyeducation.com. (2017, August 2). *Online Trading for Kids.* FamilyEducation. Retrieved November 13, 2021, from https://www.familyeducation.com/life/earning-money/online-trading-kids

Fowler, J. F. (2021, October 27). *10 Common Scams Targeted at Teens.* Investopedia. Retrieved November 11, 2021, from https://www.investopedia.com/financial-edge/1012/common-scams-targeted-at-teens.aspx

Goodwin, D. (2021, April 9). *The Way We Won: America's Economic Breakthrough During World War II*. The American Prospect. Retrieved November 12, 2021, from https://prospect.org/health/way-won-america-s-economic-breakthrough-world-war-ii/

Hayes, A. (2021, May 29). *Affluenza Definition*. Investopedia. Retrieved November 9, 2021, from https://www.investopedia.com/terms/a/affluenza.asp

Helpguidewp, Robinson, L., & Smith, M. S. (2021, July 15). *Coping with Financial Stress*. HelpGuide.Org. Retrieved November 7, 2021, from https://www.helpguide.org/articles/stress/coping-with-financial-stress.htm

History and Legacy. (n.d.). Diners Club International. Retrieved November 10, 2021, from https://www.dinersclub.com/about-us/history/

Honick, L. (2021, October 15). *The History of Currency From Bartering to the Credit Card*. Host Merchant Services. Retrieved November 10, 2021, from https://www.hostmerchantservices.com/articles/the-history-of-currency-from-bartering-to-the-credit-card/

How to become a child influencer on Instagram featuring Lovemalaha. (2019, November 19). KULTKID. Retrieved November 10, 2021, from https://kultkid.com/blogs/blog/how-to-become-a-child-influencer-on-instagram

Investment Fraud Attorneys. (n.d.). Meyer Wilson. Retrieved November 11, 2021, from https://www.investorclaims.com/library/5-common-persuasion-tactics-used-by-investment-s/

Investopedia, & Beattie, A. B. (2011, November 4). *The Evolution Of Banking*. Forbes. Retrieved November 11, 2021, from https://www.forbes.com/sites/investopedia/2011/11/03/the-evolution-of-banking/?sh=5f6b7bee6987

James Royal, Ph.D. (2021, November 12). *What Is Cryptocurrency? Here's What You Should Know*. NerdWallet. Retrieved November 13, 2021, from https://www.nerdwallet.com/article/investing/cryptocurrency-7-things-to-know

Kate, G. P. (2020, April 16). *How to Make Up to a Full-Time Income as a Video Editor*. Best of Budgets. Retrieved November 10, 2021, from https://www.bestofbudgets.com/full-time-income-as-a-video-editor/

Khan, S. (2017, December 26). *Making Children Learn The Benefits Of Budgeting From An Early Age*. Thrive Global. Retrieved November 12,

2021, from https://thriveglobal.com/stories/making-children-learn-the-benefits-of-budgeting-from-an-early-age/

Koenigsberger, H. Georg (n.d). Philip II. Encyclopedia Britannica. Retrieved November 11, 2021, from https://www.britannica.com/biography/Philip-II-king-of-Spain-and-Portugal

Nationwide, N. F. (2021, February 23). *How to Sell at a Farmers Market*. Now from Nationwide ®. Retrieved November 10, 2021, from https://blog.nationwide.com/how-to-sell-at-farmers-markets/

NOVA Online | Secrets of Making Money | The History of Money | PBS. (n.d.). Https://Www.Pbs.Org/Wgbh/Nova/Moolah/History.Html. Retrieved November 10, 2021, from https://www.pbs.org/wgbh/nova/moolah/history.html

Philosopher's Library. (n.d.). *Chinese Miniature Replicas - Around 1100 B.C.* Deepstash. Retrieved November 11, 2021, from https://deepstash.com/idea/106624/chinese-miniature-replicas-around-1100-bc

Philosopher's Library. (n.d.). Paypal and Digital Money - Around 1990. Deepstash. Retrieved November 11, 2021, from https://deepstash.com/idea/106632/paypal-and-digital-money-around-1990

Picardo, E. P. (2019, August 23). *What Is A Currency War And How Does It Work?* Investopedia. Retrieved November 12, 2021, from https://www.investopedia.com/articles/forex/042015/what-currency-war-how-does-it-work.asp

Picardo, E. P. (2021, May 1). *What Is Investing?* Investopedia. Retrieved November 13, 2021, from https://www.investopedia.com/terms/i/investing.asp

Santi, J. (2017, August 4). *The Secret to Happiness Is Helping Others.* TIME.Com. Retrieved November 8, 2021, from https://time.com/collection-post/4070299/secret-to-happiness/

Sippl, A. (2021, April 12). *10 Planning Skills Every Child Should Learn.* Life Skills Advocate. Retrieved November 13, 2021, from https://lifeskillsadvocate.com/blog/10-planning-skills-every-child-should-learn/

S.S.K. (2021, February 21). *Beware of Online Scams (Phishing, SMishing, Vishing).* Kid Safe. Retrieved November 13, 2021, from https://www.safesearchkids.com/protecting-against-online-scams-phishing-smishing-vishing/

Team, U. (2021, May 24). What is self-control? Understood.Org. Retrieved November 12, 2021, from https://www.understood.org/articles/en/self-control-what-it-means-for-kids

Teaching Guide: Appreciating Yourself - Good Character. (2020, January 17). Character Education - Social Emotional Learning - Life Skills - Lesson Plans & Curriculum. Retrieved November 11, 2021, from https://www.goodcharacter.com/elementaryschool/appreciating-yourself/

Thinking Skills: Focus. (2017, October 31). LearningWorks for Kids.
Retrieved November 13, 2021, from
https://learningworksforkids.com/educators/focus/

Thune, K. T. (2021, August 6). Investing Tips to Get Kids Started With
Mutual Funds. The Balance. Retrieved November 12, 2021, from
https://www.thebalance.com/best-mutual-funds-for-kids-2466347

What are commodity funds? (n.d.). BlackRock. Retrieved November 13,
2021, from
https://www.blackrock.com/us/individual/education/commodity-funds

Wikipedia contributors. (2021, November 8). *United States Bullion*
Depository. Wikipedia. Retrieved November 12, 2021, from
https://en.wikipedia.org/wiki/United_States_Bullion_Depository

Wikipedia contributors. (2021, November 11). *History of banking.*
Wikipedia. Retrieved November 13, 2021, from
https://en.wikipedia.org/wiki/History_of_banking

Wikipedia contributors. (2021, October 24). *Wall Street Crash of 1929.*
Wikipedia. Retrieved November 12, 2021, from
https://en.wikipedia.org/wiki/Wall_Street_Crash_of_1929

Wikipedia contributors. (2021, August 20). *History of capitalist theory.*
Wikipedia. Retrieved November 10, 2021, from
https://en.wikipedia.org/wiki/History_of_capitalist_theory

Zig Ziglar Quotes. (n.d.). BrainyQuote.com. Retrieved November 13, 2021, from BrainyQuote.com Web site:

https://www.brainyquote.com/quotes/zig_ziglar_617790